The Invading Force

by
Roberts Liardon

ALBURY PUBLISHING

Unless otherwise indicated, all Scripture quotations are taken from the *King James Version* of the Bible.

9th Printing
Over 59,000 in Print

The Invading Force
ISBN 1-88008-967-X

Copyright © 1987 by Roberts Liardon Ministries
P.O. Box 30710
Laguna Hills, California 92654

Published by ALBURY PUBLISHING
P.O. Box 470406
Tulsa, Oklahoma 74137

Spirit *Life Journal* is Roberts Liardon's "pulpit to the world." Each colorful, bi-monthly issue will challenge, encourage and enlighten you with faith-building articles on God's past "Generals," Guest Pulpit articles from ministers around the world; plus special messages and features from Roberts.

For your free subscription, write:

ROBERTS LIARDON MINISTRIES
P.O. Box 30710
Laguna Hills, CA 92654-0710

(Be sure to print your complete address, zip code or country code).

Roberts Liardon Ministries International Sales Contacts:

In England, Europe, Eastern Europe, and Scandanavia
P.O. Box 103
Knutsford
Cheshire WA169EL
England

In Asia:
Roberts Liardon Productions
Ruffles City
P.O. Box 1365
Singapore 9117

In New Zealand and Australia:
Lifeway Ministries
P.O. Box 303
Warkworth, New Zealand

Contents

1
The Move Is On

They shall run like mighty men; they shall climb the wall like men of war; and they shall march every one on his ways, and they shall not break their ranks:

Neither shall one thrust another; they shall walk every one in his path: and when they fall upon the sword, they shall not be wounded.

They shall run to and fro in the city; they shall run upon the wall, they shall climb up upon the houses; they shall enter in at the windows like a thief.

The earth shall quake before them; the heavens shall tremble: the sun and the moon shall be dark, and the stars shall withdraw their shining:

And the Lord shall utter his voice before his army: for his camp is very great: for he is strong that executeth his word: for the day of the Lord is great and very terrible; and who can abide it?

Joel 2:7-11

In these verses in Joel, we read of the great outpouring of the Holy Spirit in which we are now living. We are in the beginning of the greatest outpouring of the Holy Spirit the world has ever seen!

This move of God is going to be very different from past moves, however, because it is going to "invade" people's homes and communities. The prophet Joel is talking about an army, a force, that cannot be stopped. He talks about an army that does not break rank. When this army — made up of you and me — invades, it wins. We are going to rule this earth for God!

In order to be part of this invading force, we must change our attitude toward God. We must line up with His thinking. As I travel across North America, speaking in both small and large churches, I see a great dividing line being drawn by the Spirit of the Lord. On one side stand those who are going on with the things of God, and on the other side are those Christians who are not moving with the Lord.

Marching Orders

Also, I am beginning to see something else: Those who are going on with God have begun to get vocal about their beliefs. In other words, they have begun to "rock the boat," and many people are becoming afraid of them. Those unwilling to move on with God are beginning to withdraw from the others and say, "You are a fanatic! You are in error!"

The Word of the Lord that keeps coming to me is: "You just go ahead and invade. Go ahead and be a force that cannot be stopped. Do what God tells you to do, and let everyone else be responsible for their reactions or responses. Don't have any sleepless nights about what God tells *you* to do. Let those who don't like you or what you are doing have the sleepless nights."

Another thing the Lord has been impressing on me is that it is time for those who have a vision from God to start exercising their faith for what God has promised them. As you keep invading, God will give you the faith to cause the whole vision to happen. Do not let other people hold you back. Keep marching, keep running, because that is what God wants you to do in this day and hour. No matter what happens, if the call of God is upon your life and if God has given you a vision, concentrate totally on what He has called you to do.

People used to say to me, "Roberts, be very careful about what you say and do. You are young in the ministry. You do not have the higher education so many other preachers do. You do not have a doctorate of theology."

For awhile, I listened to them, but the Word of God kept coming to me, and He gave me this second chapter of Joel. I suggest that you read the entire chapter. Notice that in this army that cannot be stopped, the soldiers have no fear. When people hear and see *them*, the people tremble for fear because this army is such a powerful force.

If you want to be in this force, you must turn loose of the things that bind you. For example, you must be loosed from words that hold you back.

Obeying God

When God says, "Move," don't discuss it — move! When God says, "Jump," then jump! Too many believers want to discuss it. Some want to have a board meeting about it! Don't do that. When God says, "Get up and go," then get up and go. Don't ask questions. Just go! When you get to your destination, God will take care of everything.

Look at the life of Abraham. God said, "Abraham, get up from *this* country, and go over *there.*" Abraham did not know where "there" was, but he got up and left Ur of the Chaldees. He did not sit around and ask the City Council what it thought about God's instructions. Abraham just left for "there." That is what you need to do when you hear from God. Do not let anything hold you back. Do not let other religious circles hold you back from flowing with God's Spirit.

Move on into the realm of the Holy Spirit. Go on into those new worlds. Be a part of this invading force that is at work on the earth today!

God is *not* going to use people who always ask questions. He is not going to use people who are not established in the Holy Spirit. He is not going to use people who want to hold a board meeting about everything.

God *is* going to use people who hear and obey Him. This great army Joel spoke about will be comprised of such people. They are going to be people who do not understand the word no. The only thing they are going to know is when God says, "Go," they will go. They are going to have victory every time.

The reason so many churches start in the power of the Holy Spirit and then collapse is because they begin to try to organize, or put in a box, the Spirit of God. There is nothing wrong with organization as long as it is flexible enough to flow *with* the Spirit of God, but you are never to tell the Holy Spirit what to do — He tells *you* what to do.

A church should abide under the shadow of the Almighty. When God speaks, the whole church should obey. Do not question what God said, and do not worry about what other people are going to think about it. Just do it!

Losing the Fear of Man

For a long time, the Lord told me to use my little book about Heaven, *I Saw Heaven,* as an evangelistic tool. He told me to get it into as many places as I possibly could, as fast as I could.

I said, "God, that is a wild story to some people. Even though it contains Scriptures, it is almost controversial. Some religious people do not like it, especially when they know I am quite young and inexperienced. God, why don't we hold off?"

God replied, "Don't you dare. You have *got* to do it! You do not need to be ashamed of what God has given you. You have got to be a power, a force."

My greatest fears were that people were going to say I was just in the ministry for the money or else they were going to accuse me of building my ministry on this testimony of going to Heaven. (I know in my heart that those criticisms are not true.)

Then the Lord spoke to me through a woman evangelist. As we were having dinner one night, she looked up and said, "Roberts, today God gave me something for you. God has been speaking to me to get my literature into the hands of as many people as I can, as quickly as I can. I was looking through some magazines, and I saw your advertisement in one. When I saw it, the Spirit of God told me that I need to advertise, too. And this is what He told me to tell you. He said, 'Anytime I have given you a truth or moved in your life, and have told you to go give it to the people, you should not be ashamed of it. You should use every avenue to get it into the hands of people, even if you have to *force* it into their hands!' "

I got rid of all the fears of what people might think of me when my book began to be translated into different languages.

Reaching beyond your own community into the uttermost parts of the earth is a mark of this end-time move. If you are always invading and conquering lands, what your critics say will not amount to anything. By the time they start speaking against you, you will have doubled your outreach and gone on to something else.

Understand this: We live in a critical point in time. The world is coming to an end. Time is coming to a close, and the last voice must be the voice of God to the churches. No longer will there be a few "superstars." Yes, there will always be the traveling ministry, but huge churches will be used mightily now in this end-time move of God's Spirit.

Pastors, never be satisfied. Always look for new horizons. Always keep invading. Always be doing something. Be like this army in Joel that cannot be stopped. Cause the devil to fear. Cause the ungodly to fear your presence and the very name of your church. Do not fear what people say. Let them fear you.

Spiritual Strategies

The Lord also told me, "Roberts, preach what I give you, no matter how 'far out' it may sound."

If you have heard my ministry, you know that I do preach what some think are "far out" sermons, because I know there is another world that most people have not moved into yet. There is a realm in the spirit where you can walk, talk, and live. By the sovereignty of God, a few people have tapped into that realm once in a great while, but not many people want to live in it.

People do not know how to get to this realm in the spirit, and when you start preaching about these things, it rocks the boat — especially the devil's boat. He does not want people to invade the spirit world. He prefers to invade *our* world instead. He always wants to be on the offensive. Well, *we* need to be on the offensive. We need to invade *his* territory. We need to put fear in *his* heart.

When you invade, it causes faith to grow in your heart, power to come into you, and tells God that you are going to move on with Him.

I do not have much patience with people who are always "waiting on their ministry." When I get around Bible school students in particular, I do everything I can to get them to *do* something, even if it is not along the lines of their ultimate calling.

"Just do *something*," I tell them. "Go pass out tracts. Visit people in the hospitals. Start invading. Do not sit and wait for a vision from God. Do not wait for someone else to hear for you. If God tells you to do something, do it! Keep the fire burning in your heart. Continue to seek new heights. Don't digress. Always be an aggressor. Always go forward. Be a part of this army.

This aggressive attitude is what Joel prophesied about. He said that in the last days, there would arise young men and young women and old men and old women who would move in power under the mighty hand of God's Spirit.

As I have been reading and re-reading the Book of Joel, I have noticed that he was not writing about a group of people who were *defending* the city. They were *invading* the city. They were running on the walls. They were blowing trumpets. They were out there fighting in real life. That is where you need to be, as well — out where life is real. Many Christians do not know what it is to be in a battle. They do not know what it is to attack the forces of the devil. They only know what it is to defend, and defense is not fun. Attacking is fun. *When you learn to attack, you learn one of the joys of being a Christian.* If you are always defending, life gets tough. You want to quit and go someplace else.

The great preachers were always attacking. Look at Smith-Wigglesworth. He was always attacking and invading the devil's kingdom. It is fun when you are the one who starts the battle. It is fun to win. If you will start it, you will win. If you are always defending, you may lose.

You must learn spiritual strategies to use in surprise attacks against the enemy. You must learn to go up to the throne of God. You must learn how God operates in the realm of the spirit, and you must learn how to flow and work with the angels of God. I am not talking about something *imaginary.* I am talking about a realm that is very *real,* and it is in and around us today. Many Christians do not know about this realm or else they ignore it.

Do not hold back those who are going on into this realm. Whether you understand spiritual warfare or not, don't dare speak out against those who are in the invading force. God protects those who are obedient to Him.

Believe me, in this day and time, God's hand as never before is going to come to this earth to protect

His people. In the Book of Joel, we see that the wicked fear, tremble, fall, and run from the invading force. That is what is happening today: People are becoming afraid of Christians. First, however, make sure the devil is afraid of *you*. If you ever win a victory in the spirit world, you will have this victory in the natural world a few seconds later. Victory usually will come that fast.

The army Joel saw was led by the Spirit of God. According to the soldiers' natural reasoning, they did not know where they were going. Their minds did not know. Their hearts said, "Go here. Go there. Do this. Do that." You must learn to walk in faith like that to be in the invading force. You can hear all kinds of faith formulas and other good teachings on faith, but there is another realm of faith that you cannot define. That realm must be experienced; you must just walk in it.

People often ask, "How do you do such things? Why do you say such things? Where is that place? Can you tell us about it?"

I really cannot. All I can answer is to simply say, "I know it is there, but you have to get in it, you have to live in it, to know what it is like. I can only help you build a foundation. I am trying to impart to you that fire, that zeal, that strength, that *knowing* that is within my heart, so that you can rise up, invade the powers of darkness of this world, and control them with God's wisdom.

That is what God has called you to do: He wants you to rule the money of your city. He wants you to rule the political system of your city. He wants you to rule in every area. If you begin to invade the realm of the spirit in your area, you will begin to come up against the "principalities and powers," some of the most powerful forces of darkness in the earth today, not just lesser demons. Principalities and powers are strong, and they are smart. But I tell you: God is bigger, and He is smarter!

Unlimited Power

The earth must know where we Christians stand. The devil must know who we are and that we have power, because the day is coming when the prince of the powers of darkness is going to stand on one side of a stage and God's people are going to stand on the other. We had better know that we have power with our Creator.

We had better know that when we speak, God is going to move. The powers of darkness are going to be able to perform signs and wonders. (2 Thess. 2:9.) They are going to be able to do unusual things. We have to have power to control them. *We have to be a force with unlimited power.* Most Christians today, like Samson, know the limits of their power. We must get to the place, however, where we feel *no* limits, where we will *know* that all power is given unto us.

God has issued the call that this power is available, and we can walk in the realm of the spirit. Many people, however, are trying to use formulas to achieve this power. There is nothing wrong with sermons that give steps to success, but you cannot give step one, two, and three to get to the place I am talking about.

The place is different for every person. Every responsibility is different, but whatever it costs, whatever it takes, it is worth it. Give up all and seek the Kingdom of God. Give up all and work for God.

We are coming to a critical time in the realm of the spirit and in the world. This age is coming to a close, and we need to be busy invading. We have to let the earth know that there is a God and that He is alive and well. The only way this is going to happen is when enough people declare, "I know God reigns. See this?" BAM — and there is a miracle.

We need to get to that place where the power of God is flowing. Power is what we need, not talk. The power of God is available to any believer. God has no favorites. The only reason there are "superstars" in God's work is because so few people are willing to pay the price to get there.

What God gave some people in the Bible and down through history is available to us today if we will pay the price to get it. The great people of the past were people who invaded. They knew how to work with angels, and they surrounded themselves with people who had that same spirit of invading.

Look at Joshua: He was always looking ahead, always planning the invasion. If you have a Joshua as a pastor, get behind him and join him in the battle. Never speak against him. Always pray for him.

One of the main reasons churches fall is that, when God begins to move, the devil encourages some of the members to begin criticizing what the pastor is doing. Of course, they do not realize it is the devil. They think those critical thoughts are their own, and they receive them and act on them. Don't be guilty of this.

Believe me, when a pastor first starts a church, he will make mistakes. When you criticize him, you give the enemy ammunition. The devil hears and acts on the words you say, just as God acts on what you say. Do not say, "The pastor is going to fail." That gives the devil another degree of power to use against the church. Instead, go home, get in your prayer closet, and say, "God, if I am wrong, change me. If my pastor is wrong, change him; but, God I want this church to succeed for your glory."

Be careful what you do and say. Put your whole heart in it, and do what the Bible says. Do not try to change things to fit the way *you* believe. Do not speak out against any man or woman. Just walk in divine love. That will cause the power to come, that will prove to God that you are real.

God's power is not going to come to a person who is playing games and doing what he wants to do. His power is going to come to those walking according to His laws. The New Testament has laws and regulations in it as well as the Old Testament. Many people say, "But we are under grace. We can do anything we want to do." That is what you think! God says we are to walk in love, but how many do this? God gave us certain commandments, and He did not add, "If you *want* to, walk in love." No, He said, "Do it!" So many people do not want to do what God says. They want to play games and do what *they* want to do.

To be part of that great army Joel wrote about, you must obey the laws and rules of the Holy Spirit without question. You must walk in them with all your power and might. This does not take great faith. You can have a small amount of faith, add hope to it, and direct it to the throne of God, then He will take it and use it to your benefit.

Many Christians are trying to achieve things in their own strength. They want to be *golden* or *silver* vessels, when God simply is looking for *human* vessels, *yielded* vessels. That is what you must be. You do not need a university education to serve God. You do not need to be wealthy to serve God. You can serve God if you have an education or money, of course. The point is that in either case, with or without worldly goods and knowledge, to serve God means being a yielded vessel.

Others may try to discourage you by saying, "You don't know this. You don't have that. You have only been a Christian for a short time." God is not looking at all those things, however, He is looking at the yieldedness, or the obedience, of your heart.

If you can learn to live in a state of yieldedness to the Holy Spirit, you can accomplish great things for God. *One of the greatest secrets of the Kingdom of God is learning to yield to the mighty Third Person of the Trinity.*

Summoned to Be Part of a Great Army

We are being called, summoned, to be part of a great army that Joel says will not be stopped. The soldiers in that army are to run like mighty men. They shall climb over walls like men of war. They shall march and not break rank. The spear shall go into them, and they will not be wounded. What a good guarantee! Usually, when people go to war, they know they will face tragedy and death. In this army, when we become a part of God's invading force, we will not be hurt. (Joel 2:8.) We will always be protected, and we will cause fear in the camp of the enemy.

No wonder worldly people fight those who are going on with God: It causes the demons in them to scream and quake. Demons should know when we walk down the street that we have power. The presence of Jesus in us should cause them to scream and come out of people. That is the way it should be, and it is possible to achieve this. You can have this power, but it is up to you to get it. I know most of you think that it is for special people or else you think you have to do special things to get that kind of power. No, you just do what God tells you to do, and you can have this power of the Holy Spirit.

When Jesus walked up to a man who had a legion of demons in him, those demons knew who Jesus was. They said, "Son of God, why have you come here to torment us?" That is the way it should be with Christians, and that is the way it is going to be.

Many are tired of hearing that this next move of God is going to be great — but it *is*. They are tired of hearing that Jesus is coming soon, because generation after generation has heard this since He went back to heaven. Many people now alive have heard that message personally for fifty years. They have almost given up faith and hope, but He *is* coming soon! Do not ever lose that hope. Keep it within your heart. Let there forever be a knowing within you that God's power and glory are coming. Jesus is coming soon, and we will be leaving this world. In the meantime, we have to be a force, a power, that cannot be stopped or quenched, that is always going forward and never resting. There is no time to rest.

The Book of Joel never talks about a time when that army relaxed and took a vacation. It never says they went to Hawaii for a week. Believe me, if God does send you to Hawaii, you are not going there to lie on the beach. You might walk on the beach, but you will probably find someone to witness to or to cast the devil out of.

God is going to do the unusual in this day and time. The Book of Isaiah talks about the *strange* acts of God. I am longing to see them. We have seen a few acts of God, but we have not seen anything yet. Our eyes will behold the mighty outpouring of God's Spirit.

No matter how large your church may become, remember that it is the members who carry the church, not the guest speakers. It is you who must become the invading force.

The fivefold ministry gifts are the leaders of God's end-time army. They visit your church, give the orders, and exhort the troops. Then they move on to another "camp" and do the same thing. It is the "troops," however, who must carry out those orders and do the actual invading. The leaders must go where the light is dim, the Gospel is not heard, and the power is not known.

God said to me once, "While you are young, you are going to go to all the rough places."

I replied, "I don't want to go there. I want to go to Europe where it's nice."

He said, "You are not going there until you get old."

I said, "Well, that's nice. Your mercy endureth forever, Lord."

And He said, "Yes, it does."

Most of my overseas invitations are from rough places. They are always from those Third World countries where they are about to go to war.

21

When you are friends with God, you can talk to Him about anything, and He understands what you mean. The reason some Christians cannot do that is because they do not know God. You need to know Him. He is my Friend, Who lives with me and walks and talks with me. I know what He likes and what He dislikes, and He knows my heart. I can look up to Heaven and say anything, and He will just smile at me. I have never offended Him by joking with Him.

Many people misunderstand this statement, but those who do understand do not have "common" sense. In other words, to understand God, you have to get over into the world of the spirit. That is one reason God is going to use young people in this new move: They do not have "common" sense. They do not understand the word *no*, they only understand *go*. They are going to run in the glory of God. They are going to go to presidents and kings and say, "Thus saith the Lord." Believe me, that is one reason why the Holy Spirit inspired Joel to say that in the last days young men shall see visions.

God is moving. God is creating more visions. God is speaking to His people as never before. We need to open our ears and hear what He is saying, and then move to perform it, not sit back and discuss it. Once you are certain the voice speaking is God, discussion would be of the devil. If God says, "Jump through that wall," and there is no hole there, just start jumping. By the time you hit the wall, there will be a hole there. It is God's business to put the hole there. You just start jumping — that is called faith. That is called invading. That is where we need to be.

The Balanced Christian Life

Also understand that there must be a balance to everything we hear. *We must be able to discern the spirits, because as soon as God speaks, the devil also is going to speak.* He is going to try to deceive us. If we are led by the Third Person of the Trinity, however, we will not get into error. Jesus said that the Holy Spirit will guide us into all truth, not partial truth. The Holy Spirit will keep us where we are supposed to be. His everlasting arms will reach down and help us. We must make sure our hearts are clean, our lives are pure, and our motives are right.

I believe the day will come when believers will move with such sensitivity in the realm of the Holy Spirit that there will not be as many mistakes. There will be perfection. When there is no error, when there is only a hunger and a thirst after God, the Spirit of God will fall upon us. He will move in our hearts and give us what we desire.

There is more to the Christian life than most people think. After we are saved, we have a battle to fight. We have a war to win, and we are in it whether we want to be or not. We are just like the young people in modern Israel. Most of them, as soon as they are old enough, go straight into military training.

As soon as we are born again, we go into "boot camp" also. Then we are sent out to fight. Many Christians deliberately try to flunk boot camp, however. They do not want to go fight. They want to stay where it is easy, so they end up defending the camp.

Learning to attack is a lot more fun, because God needs no defense. He is His own defense. He needs people to attack the enemy for Him. He needs you to go forth to conquer, to be a voice, to carry a standard for Him, to say, "This is the way it is going to go" and then to have the power to perform it.

God's power cannot be unlimited in this world until we learn to do what He says, until we prove to Him that we are real, until we walk the floor in prayer, pay our tithes, pray for the sick, and pass our tracts — even when no one is saved or healed. Most people do not want to do that. When they pray for the sick, they want everyone to be healed. If it does not happen every time, you have to keep on praying. That is called invading.

When you invade, do not have second thoughts and retreat — just invade. You are in it to the death, not your death but the devil's. You need to have the attitude of "I am going to win, or I am going to die trying."

Spiritual Violence

The Book of Matthew talks about the violent taking the Kingdom by force. (Matt. 11:12.) Violent people do not have common sense. When people are violent enough, they always win. When we think of violence, however, we usually think of crime, of something that is wrong. But if we get violent for God and use this *spiritual* violence as a positive force, we will build our churches. We will build our television stations. We will own our own satellites. We will own land. We will own everything we want and be happy. We will just invade the whole place. We will set captives free, heal the sick, and take our authority back from Satan, and that is the way it should be.

In other words, until end-time prophecy comes to pass, let us rule over the forces of darkness through the name of Jesus. Let us be a power. Let us be a force.

If you do not want to go on with God, then go home, because you are going to get upset with those who are doing something. I would rather not hear you complain, because you may be judged. The first thing God usually does in a church, when someone speaks out against what He is doing, is remove them. He will deal with them in mercy first, then He will deal with them in judgment. He will remove them, because this army must be the last army — and it *will* succeed.

My generation is a generation of preachers. Many people just do not know it yet. One way they are going to find out is by people like me telling them and then letting them worry about it. Too often, we are afraid of what people are going to think and say. Forget it! Let it go. Let them worry about it. Let them have the sleepless nights. You shout the victory. You shout up and down the aisles of the churches.

Let the earth know who God is by performing miracles and proclaiming Him on the streets. Let the people have the truth. Don't hold back. Give it everything you have. Invade the world of darkness with all your might, and take back what belongs to you.

If you are in poverty, get violent about it and get rich. Enjoy prosperity, and let your critics cope with it. If you are sick, get violent about it, and pray the sickness out of yourself. If other sick people get upset because you are well, let them keep their sicknesses. One day they will wake up and want to be like you. After they decide they want to get rid of all the demons that are causing their sickness, they will come to you and ask, "Please teach me how to do it." Believe me, they will.

If you want power with God, get it. Let those who do not like it cope with it. They will come back to you. They will say, "Teach me. Teach me."

When I first began my ministry, no one thought I could make it because I was so young, but I am still here. They are still coming to see me, but now they are saying, "Teach me. Teach me." I say, "Yield." But they do not understand.

The simplest things sometimes are the most complex for believers to understand. *God is simple, and the things of the Lord are so simple that most people miss them.* It is so simple to get the gifts of the Holy Spirit. You do not have to achieve anything. Just yield. "Yield" is a simple word and a simple action. *Get helpless as the gifts come. Just be a yielded person.* Give the glory to God and have fun.

This Christian walk and the witnessing that belongs to the Christian lifestyle are easy when you are attacking and obeying. Things get difficult if you are just defending and not attacking. I have noticed that when some people witness to someone, they do it in a defensive manner. If they are witnessing to someone who is not Spirit filled, they start defending tongues, for example. Forget defending. Just proclaim the baptism of the Holy Spirit as a truth, and let them find it. Do not give a definition to everything you do. Don't worry about it. Just do what needs to be done. Get free from that bondage, and let other people cope with their own beliefs.

Why Be Prosperous?

Listen to what Joel says in chapter 2, verses 10 and 11:

> The earth shall quake before them; the heavens shall tremble: the sun and the moon shall be dark, and the stars shall withdraw their shining:
>
> And the Lord shall utter his voice before his army: for his camp is very great: for he is strong that executeth his word: for the day of the Lord is great and very terrible; and who can abide it?

This is a powerful chapter. Verses 25 and 26 speak of restoration and prosperity:

> And I will restore to you the years that the locust hath eaten, the cankerworm, and the caterpillar, and the palmerworm, my great army which I sent among you.
>
> And ye shall eat in plenty, and be satisfied.

That is for you and me. No longer will the Church have needs that are not met. The day will come when we will be multi-million-dollar organizations with enough money to buy anything we want and to invent anything we need. It is going to come to that, so if you do not like a church to be rich, go find a poor one. We see in this second chapter of Joel that the Lord promises to bless us. In verse 26, we saw where we would eat in plenty.

We are moving into the most prosperous time the Christian army has ever seen, because we are beginning to win for once. We are beginning to understand what belongs to us. Let those who are bound with religious tradition cope with tradition. Let them live in the poverty, and let them enjoy their demons — if they can. As for me, I am going to enjoy all that the Lord has for me. **Forget not all his benefits,** the Word says (Ps. 103:2). Most people reject God's benefits when they arrive at the door. They say, "I don't want them." Well, send them to me.

Many people are worried that if they start invading, start doing something out of the ordinary, their ordinary support will crumble, their popularity will disappear, and people will speak out against them. Yes, those things happen if you start going with God. The financial support that was promised you from the natural probably *will* fall away, but you must remember that God is your Source.

Evangelist Oral Roberts has said "God is your Source" so many times over television that people may not really hear what is being said. Nevertheless, it is true. You must understand that God *is* your Source. We look not unto man but unto God, Who is our Source, our Creator, our Provider, and the One we call in the time of trouble. We ask of Him, and we receive. God has a million people He can move upon to get your needs met. We do not need to worry. We need to have faith in God. Jesus even said when He was on the earth: **Let not your heart be troubled, neither let it be afraid** (John 14:27). Do not doubt God, and do not worry.

Also, do not let your checkbook hold you back. If you cannot give, mow the church lawn. Do *something.* Start *somewhere.* When we think "offering," we usually think of money; and, believe me, money is important. It is going to take millions and millions of dollars to take this Gospel to every creature, and it has got to come from this army. You have to start somewhere. A lot of people think, "If I can't give $1,000, I am not going to give."

If you think you are poor, you should see the Africans to whom I preach. They live in little huts with one light — a string with a light bulb. There are holes in their roads the size of a car. People are dying in

Africa, and their families are being massacred by the new armies taking over in many countries. The people are not allowed to own anything anymore.

I decided to teach them how to prosper, and the devil ran true to form — he sent a negative thought before I could preach a positive one. He said, "They do not have anything to give. Prosperity does not work here in Africa."

I said, "That is a lie!" So I began to teach the Africans, "If you do not have anything, if you cannot bring food to the pastor to give to the needy, get a rock. Get a plant. Get a leaf. Get *something*! Do something for the church. Knit socks for the pastor's son. Paint a picture, even if it is ugly. Hang it up somewhere. Do something. Let God know you are real. Let the devil know that you have faith in God. Tell the three worlds — Heaven, Earth, and Hell — that you are going on with a great God. You have to do something; you cannot always wait for your day of prosperity to dawn. *Help* it dawn. *Cause* it to dawn.

So the Africans got their rocks and started polishing them. They began bringing things to church. They brought me a mat and said, "You can put it by your bed, and you can kneel down on it." They started to do something. They did not ask questions. They just moved. That is where Africans have it over Americans. Their situation is so critical that if they do not do something, they will die.

Walking by Faith

It is time to get back to the simple things of God. So many people want new revelations, and believe me, we will get new revelations because God has fun enlightening our eyes. Remember, no matter how many revelations you get on faith — faith is still faith. It is not complicated. Just believe in the Creator. Learn to rely on unseen resources. Learn to rely on an unseen Person. That is faith!

In other words, learn to reach and grab something you cannot feel. Learn to walk where there is no ground. Learn to accept victory when it seems there is no victory. That is faith.

Many of you stand on the threshold of taking the first stop toward fulfilling that vision God has given you, but you have things in your lives that the devil is trying to use against you — family problems, social problems, emotional problems, or financial problems.

God says, "Have faith in Me, because I will help you. I know what I am doing better than you do. I know what is going on. My eyes go to and fro throughout the earth. They see everything. My hand is all-powerful. It knows no limits."

Get Free From the Past

God is willing to work with you, if you will have faith in Him. Do not let your heart be troubled. Have faith in God. Get forgiven of those things that were problems to you in the past. Let them go into the sea of God's forgetfulness. Once they are forgiven, do not ever remember them.

If the devil tries to throw them up to you, invade his territory, attack him, and say, "No! My sins are gone forever. I am free because of the blood of Jesus Christ." Hit the devil with chapter and verse from the Bible. Be free in the glory and the Spirit of God.

It is vital that no matter what your past life was, you realize that you have been forgiven. If you have problems, *God is the Answer.* God is the great *I Am.* He is the God of the *now*, not tomorrow or yesterday, but right now. God cares for you. He loves you. If you have been through a divorce, if you have had a bankruptcy, if you were in sin — no matter what happened — God's grace is almighty. Jesus' blood cleanses us from all sin. When you say, "God, forgive me," He rushes to forgive you. He says in His Word, "Before you call, I will answer" (Isa. 65:24). Believe me, He is just like that. He is a God of His Word.

Forget the past. Look up, and see new horizons. See your destiny. Do not look at what is behind you. That is the reason the Spirit of God told the Apostle Paul to write these words: **I press toward the mark for the prize of the high calling of God in Christ Jesus** (Phil. 3:14). Notice that the Holy Spirit did not call it the *low* calling but the *high* calling. If it is a *high* calling, you have to look *up* into it. Forgetting those things that are behind, look *forward*, press *into* — that is where you need to be.

The Invading Force

Jesus invaded. The Apostle Paul invaded. The disciples and the apostles invaded. When the apostles came to town, the people said, "Oh, no! Here come those men who have turned the world upside down" (Acts 17:6). That is the way we need to be. We need to be even greater than the early Church.

I was once ministering in Missouri with a prophet of God. We visited a very good church, but the pastor was extremely cautious. The bigger the church gets, the more cautious the pastor needs to be. I can understand that, and I believe that is of God. But the Spirit of God led us to that church. We did not know they did not believe that Christians can have demons.

Demons can get in your *mind* and in your *body,* but they cannot get in your *spirit,* if you are a Christian. If they oppress your mind, they will cramp your spirit. You need to be set free, and you need someone to help you get set free.

I was preaching away in this church, and the Spirit of God said, "Give a call for deliverance." About a thousand people were there, and I thought perhaps a hundred at the most might respond — but more than seven hundred people got in the prayer line.

For at least two hours, the prophet of the Lord and I cast out demons — and not just one demon out of each person. Some of those people had several in them. They were born again, Spirit filled, but they did not understand why they were not happy. The devil had stolen their joy from them.

Later, we discovered that we had created a ruckus in the spirit world by setting those people free. After the service, we went to a restaurant. After you have cast out thousands of demons, you are tired and hungry. You get tired because it is warfare, even though you jump for joy.

We sat in a private room shielded from the other rooms in the restaurant by blinds. We had been there for about twenty minutes, talking about what God had done, when two young women walked in who had not been in the meeting. They sat down in the next room, peeked at us through the blinds, and the demons in them began to say, "There they are!" At first, it did not dawn on me what they were talking about.

Then they began to holler and make fun of us. They screamed, "Those are the ones who hurt us tonight. Those are the ones we need to be careful of. We need to be careful of them, because they are powerful."

When you become an invading force, things like that will begin to happen to you, and you will know you are a big threat to the kingdom of darkness. It is time to rejoice when demons get upset and begin to scream at you.

That experience proved to me that I was on track. Believe me, when you start invading, you will become known in the natural world as well as in the spirit realm. There will be battles against your family, your church, and every aspect of your life. Remember! The Greater One lives inside you.

You have power over all the works of the devil. You are mighty on this earth because God has given you His power to perform His works on this earth. My friends, our generation is the generation that Joel and Peter prophesied about. We are that invading force. This revival is not like all the others. The truths of all the others will be in this revival, but this is a new one. All the revivals of the past were defensive, but we are going to attack.

We are going to be an invading force.

2

UNENDING REVIVAL

What is revival? A revival is experiencing an intense presence of God on the earth. Revival is literally feeling the presence of God walking up and down the aisles of churches. A revival is when men come into contact with an invisible Being, and they cannot deny that there is a real, unseen Force called God in their midst.

In the early days of creation, Adam walked in the Spirit of God and set the trend for all subsequent moves of God's Spirit. The Lord once told me, "I have always started the moves, but men always stopped them. I never designed for revival to end. I started it on the day of creation. I meant for it to last forever on the planet called Earth. But because of the fall of man, men stopped revival, and it is difficult for them to get back in the flow of it again."

Those who live in the realm of the spirit live in constant revival, because the spirit realm is in a constant move, a constant revival.

When men turn their hearts back to God in a new obedience, a new commitment, revival will begin to spread across the earth. When men get desperate, when they start crying out for God and travel to the realm of the spirit, revival will break out.

As we saw, God never designed for revival to end. He meant for revival to continue forever. Revival stops when Christians get lazy. In the days to come, however, the revivals of the past and the truths brought forth in those moves will combine with a new blast of God's glory. It will be the greatest outpouring of the Holy Spirit that the world has ever seen or felt. The gates of Hell cannot prevail against this move that is coming to the Earth.

No religious organization will organize it out of existence this time. No one will preach it to death. It is coming, and it is coming full force.

Revival Now

People in Heaven are very much aware of the happenings on Earth. They are very much aware of what you are doing for the Kingdom. They even pray for the saints who are on the Earth. The Book of Ephesians states that we are *one family* in Heaven and in Earth. We are not two separate families, we are one. What the family in Heaven has, we on Earth can have: That same Presence, that same peace, that same power belongs to us on Earth. We do not have to wait to go to Heaven to enjoy God's presence or power. They belong to us now.

Many people, however, do not want to pay the price for God's glory. They want to ride on the coat tails of other people, but coat tails are becoming short. No longer can somebody "piggyback" you into God's glory.

Some will call this coming revival a selfish revival, because it is going to be only for those who will seek it. This revival is not going to come to men like past revivals did. In God's sovereign moves of the past, He always met man, but I believe that this new move has come as far as it is going to come. Now *we must go to it* in order to be in it. That is the difference between this outpouring and all the outpourings of the past.

That is what is causing the great separation we presently see among the people of God. Many are puzzled because there is no confusion or strife in this new move. They do not understand that when you get in the flow of revival, there cannot be confusion or strife. Slowly but surely, this age is coming to an end. God's moves in this age are getting less frequent. Because of this, we must go to where the move of God is. We must go into the world of the spirit.

Sermons That Change Men's Lives

I do not understand preachers who say they can only preach fifteen minutes. Believe me, if you are called, you can preach at least an hour. If you have done your homework, you can preach at least two hours. When I lecture in Bible schools, I have fifty-five minutes to deliver my two-hour sermon. The students just look at me. They cannot take notes fast enough. They say, "How can you talk that fast?" I reply, "It does not come through my head. It comes out of my heart." That is the big difference.

Sermons that will change men's lives are not educational "one, two, three" sermons. They are heartfelt, Holy Spirit sermons, sermons born out of hours of intercession for the people to whom we are to minister.

Success does not come to those who have perfect words, movements, and pulpit etiquette. Success comes to those who have gotten hold of God Almighty. When men and women like that just walk out on the platform and say, "Hello," the power of God falls. That is what the Earth needs today. The people of the world, and even people in dying churches, are not looking for another three-point sermon. They are looking for an unlimited move of the Holy Spirit.

Heaven places no limits or boundaries on the moving of the Holy Spirit. The presence of God flows and does anything it wants to in Heaven. There should never be limits or boundaries on the flow of God's Spirit in your church or your life, either.

God Is Not Weird

The flow of the Spirit of God should be loose, but not weird. God is not weird, and He does not like weird believers who claim that their weirdness is "walking in the Spirit." I am 100 percent against people who say they are in the Spirit when they actually are in the flesh or the mind. They are weird! They will not listen to someone who acts normally, someone who is in the Spirit.

Just because I do not roll down the aisle with them, they think I am not in the Spirit. Well, I do not "roll" down aisles. God has to knock me down aisles. I am not against the *movings* of the Holy Spirit. I am not against the *unusual.* I am not even against the *strange,* but I am totally against the *weird.* God does not bless weirdness, and He does not bless flakiness.

There will be a great deal of weirdness in the new glory move, if people who are real do not stand up when someone does something out of the flesh — or influenced by a demon — and declare, "That is not of God. Change!"

There must be an authority or a standard established in this new move of God, and if something does not meet that standard, it should not be received as having come from God. All the past moves of God failed because of people who got weird, people who went to extremes, and others who went off and did what *they* wanted.

The Secret of the Next Move

When you get to the place where you start telling the Holy Spirit what to do, He takes off. You do not tell God what to do, He tells *you* what to do. Also, you cannot manufacture the gifts or moving of the precious Third Person of the Trinity. It cannot be done. In this new move we are coming into, we have to be so careful that we do not grieve the Person of the Holy Spirit, because *He is the secret of this next move of God.* We have to become His very, very best friend. We have to know how to walk with Him and to talk with Him. We cannot afford to make one wrong move or speak one wrong word when the Holy Spirit is moving.

If you stand up to give a message in tongues or an interpretation, make sure it comes from the heart of God and not from your own heart. That is one of the things that causes the Holy Spirit to lift, and He might be gone for two months. We are moving into a very intense place, a realm of the Spirit where we have to be obedient. We have to know the Holy Spirit. We cannot do our own thing or try to get popular. The only One Who can get popular is the Lord Jesus Christ.

Some people just do not know any better, I realize that. Yet there are those who do know better but who stand up and give a nice word that is not for the entire congregation but for their own hearts. When someone gets out of line like that, it grieves the Holy Spirit. We have to learn how to work with the Third Person of the Trinity.

He is the One Jesus spoke about in John 16 when He told His disciples He was going away, but He would send them the Comforter. John 16:13 says, **Howbeit when he, the Spirit of truth, is come, he will guide you into all truth.** Not partial truth, *all* truth.

Flesh or Spirit?

We have to learn to listen to the Holy Spirit's wooings and teachings so that we will not take the wrong path or do the wrong thing. We stand at a crossroads in our relationship with God. No longer will He bless those who get in the flesh. No longer will He bless those who call the flesh "spirituality." He will withdraw His presence and go where people are truly hungry, truly willing to learn and flow with the Holy Spirit. He will go where there are no personalities trying to be popular.

God's personality is the only personality that should ever get any glory. It is not men who bring the moves of God. It is not even men who carry the moves. It is the Holy Spirit Who brings revival and keeps it going as long as people keep yielding and humbling themselves and saying, "God, whatever . . . ."

There is a stirring within me. I have studied Church history for about seven years. I have studied the moves of Wesley, Luther, the Voice of Healing organization, and many others, and I have seen how many preachers fell. Then I look at this move we are entering into, knowing it will be the greatest move the earth will ever see, and I cannot keep quiet. I cannot allow people to do what they want to in the flesh, claiming they are doing it in the name of God. If it is *not* of God, they must be corrected. They must be told to keep quiet and sit down for the sake of the outpouring of the Holy Spirit.

We have to have a standard. You pastors and evangelists must have the manhood and womanhood to stand up for God, to stand up for what is right, and to come against what is wrong. Do not allow your church to go off the deep end. Do not allow your people to rule you. God has you over them. You are the one who is head of that congregation, so you tell your sheep what to do. Tell them, "*This* is the moving of God, and *that* is of the flesh — change!"

We have to understand how the Holy Spirit moves. The way He moves throughout Heaven must become the way He moves throughout Earth. In the prayer services in Heaven, no one tries to become the leader or director. They gather together in the unity of faith and the Spirit, joined in the divine love that is in their hearts. They look toward the throne room of God, and as the songs within them begin to swell, no one is trying to outsing the others. No one is saying, "I danced better than you." They are flowing together to make one voice and one sound that is heard throughout all of Heaven, making the heart of God jump for joy.

We on earth must get to that unity of the spirit for this outpouring of the Holy Spirit to flow as it is supposed to and for the miracles to happen as they are supposed to. We must have that standard in line with the Holy Spirit. We cannot do what we want to do. We cannot try to be popular. We must promote the Lord Jesus Christ, let Him be the popular Person, let Him be the personality, and let Him receive all the glory, honor, praise, and worship.

The Importance of Being Yielded

As I look *into* people in a congregation, I see those who have flowed with the mighty hand of God, and I see others who have flowed only partially in the Spirit. We must get totally into the flow of the Spirit and learn to yield ourselves to the Third Person of the Trinity. He is the very secret of the power of the Trinity. He is the One Who causes people to be healed. It is His power that does it. No one else is the Healer. People who have miracles in their services are yielded to Him. They know better than anyone else that they do not heal. It is God Who heals as the Holy Spirit flow through them.

We need to become doors without locks, windows that are always open. We have to be able to say to the Holy Spirit, "Here I am. Flow with Me. Do what You want. I will go. I will say. I will be quiet. I will be still. Whatever You desire, Holy Spirit, I will do for the promotion of the Kingdom of God."

We do not have to touch people to get them healed. We do not even have to direct a prayer to a specific person to get him or her healed. If we learn to let the Holy Spirit speak and flow through our very being, He will heal people as we proclaim the Good News. It is not by our might, nor is it by our power. It is by the Spirit of the Most High that it is going to be done. (Zech. 4:6.)

We stand at a place where we have to humble ourselves. I hate to say this, but I am going to say it anyway: Many people are seeking personal popularity. They think if they can get on the platform or if they can give a message in tongues and get recognized, God will use them more. If you seek popularity, God cannot use you.

Just sit there and say, "God, I am yielded. Whatever You want is fine with me." If He decides to use you, fine. If not, fine.

When I first started in the ministry, people were always asking me, "What is your secret? How do you go out on that stage and preach those wild sermons? What is the secret of walking into a congregation and having half the congregation falling under the power when you say, 'Hello'? What is the secret?"

The secret is that God is looking for holy, yielded vessels to use.

That is why it is necessary for us to have a relationship with the Holy Spirit. We have to learn to know Him. Of course, we also must learn of Jesus — don't misunderstand me — but remember Jesus' words in John 16:

> **Nevertheless I tell you the truth; It is expedient for you that I go away: for if I go not away, the Comforter will not come unto you; but if I depart, I will send him unto you.**
>
> **And when he is come, he will reprove the world of sin, and of righteousness, and of judgment;**
>
> **Of sin, because they believe not on me;**
>
> **Of righteousness, because I go to my Father, and ye see me no more;**
>
> **Of judgment, because the prince of this world is judged.**

I have yet many things to say unto you, but ye cannot bear them now.

Howbeit when he, the Spirit of truth, is come, he will guide you into all truth: for he shall not speak of himself; but whatsoever he shall hear, that shall he speak: and he will shew you things to come.

He shall glorify me: **for he shall receive of mine, and shall shew it unto you.**

John 16:7-15

This is not saying that you cannot commune with Jesus; however, you must understand that the Holy Spirit is our Teacher. People want the Holy Spirit to flow in their lives and ministries, but often they try to accomplish that by their own achievements. God is not impressed by our achievements! *Yieldedness and humility attract God to a person.*

Let us look at the life of Smith Wigglesworth, who was an uneducated plumber whose wife had to teach him to read. He stammered, stuttered, and could not speak proper English, but when the Holy Spirit fell on him, Smith Wigglesworth would yield to the Spirit and speak as well as an English professor.

We must learn what it is to yield to the Holy Spirit like this. We must learn that it is not a magnetic personality or a great organization, it is the Holy Spirit flowing through yielded vessels that brings revival. Organizations may come out of revival and famous personalities may spring forth from it, but the key is always the Holy Spirit flowing through yielded individuals.

The Importance of Being Humble

Never build your life or ministry on an experience. You can share your experience and help many people, but that experience will not carry you through the storms of life. What will carry you through the storms of life is understanding and cooperating with the Trinity and the Word of God.

Never deviate from the Holy Bible. Then you will never get so spiritual that you will outdo the Bible. You will never get so high and mighty that you think you know more than Matthew, Mark, Luke, and John. You will never get so popular that you do not need to listen to the Holy Spirit. You will never tell the Holy Spirit what to do. You will wait for Him to tell *you* what to do.

The Holy Spirit is to be to us today what Jesus was to His disciples. Jesus taught them, "This is the way you should go." When they deviated from that way, He said, "Stop! Woe be unto you. Satan, get off them!"

The Holy Spirit corrects you the same way. The first thing He does is speak to your heart, to impress upon you, "This is not right. Don't do that. That is not of Me." He does overlook ignorance because His love is so great, and His mercy endures forever. So He will plead with you, "Please, please, don't do it. Please, go this way. Don't go that way." He will beg you because His love for you is so great. You must learn to listen to these wooings, these impressions, from the Holy Spirit, because you cannot continue to do whatever you want to do and keep the presence of the Holy Spirit in your life.

In the past, certain preachers have acted as if they were superstars of the religious world. Two noted preachers actually claimed to be Elijah. As soon as they did this, they began to fall, and their falls were very hard.

We need no more failures in the ministry, especially in this move into which we are entering. We need no more disaster cases in the ministry. When someone falls, it is a mark against the Church. It hinders the world from seeing Jesus. It is like a knife slashing the very heart of our God, because once you yield yourself to God, He takes out a guarantee on your life. He says, "Heaven, we can trust this person. He is committed."

Then God starts pouring out the power. He starts pouring out the glory. He starts opening doors of utterance to you, putting you before great and mighty men and giving you influence and divine favor. As long as you use that influence to promote the Kingdom of God and the moving of the Holy Spirit in the Earth, your anointing, your promotions, and the outpouring of the Holy Spirit in your services will grow greater.

If you start saying, "Look at me, look at what I can do," you might become like Samson. He woke up one morning without any power, because he had been fooling around in the wrong world. When his enemies came to get him, Samson shook himself and tried to use his supernatural strength, but there was no strength. He cried as they took him away.

I have seen many ministers grace the pulpit, and as they began to speak, they shook themselves — but there was nothing. They said, "Hello," and there was no power. They went back to their nice little three-point sermons that were dead and dried up, and they dwindled away. Some who lost their anointing died and went to Hell because they backslid against God. They got mad at God and screamed, "Why have You forsaken me?" They did not have enough sense to understand that they had forsaken Him when they deviated from the way they should have gone.

They took the power and began using it for self-gain. You can do that for only so long until the judgment of God will come. That judgment will be equal to your anointing — the stronger the anointing, the stronger the judgment.

Brother So-and-So's power was known throughout the earth. It used to be that when he came to town, if you could get to the services, God would meet you there. He would speak to you. He would heal the sick and save the lost.

Today, people still come by the thousands and fill the auditoriums. Brother So-and-So comes to the podium, opens the service as usual, and the excitement is raging high. As he begins to preach, however, the excitement begins to decrease. People wonder, "What is the matter with Brother So-and-So? Well, he must be tired. He has been on the mission field, and he is so exhausted."

He comes to town again next year, and the same thing happens again. People say, "Well, what is wrong now? Maybe he is under persecution." But when you are under persecution, that is the time you should glory the most. That is when the glory should be the greatest. That is when God says, "He is my servant. Watch what I do in behalf of his words!"

And the people wonder.

Knowing the Holy Spirit

You need not grieve the Holy Spirit. You need not move out of the shadow of the Almighty. Do not simply visit the world of the spirit. Go there to abide under the shadow of the Almighty. Learn to live in the presence of the Trinity. Learn to walk and to talk with them. Let the things of this world drop off. Let your eyes no longer look downward, but let them look upward into the presence of the Most High. Let your desires be on the things that are above and not on the things that are beneath.

Know that no tape or book will ever promote a ministry. No popular man who takes you under his wing and promotes your ministry will cause you to succeed. The only thing that will cause any ministry or layperson to succeed in what they are called to do is being yielded in prayer and in speaking to the people of the Lord. It is not men's words that God wants you to speak. It is His words the people need to hear, and God wants you to speak.

The only way you will get those sermons is by learning to yield yourself to the Holy Spirit. Those who work with you also must learn to flow in the unity of the Spirit. Where strife is, there is no order or move of the Holy Spirit. One wrong song can cause the power of God to lift. One wrong action can cause the glory of God to lift; however, one right action can cause the power to fall. That is why you must know the desire of the Holy Spirit for that service.

Learn to know the Person of the Holy Spirit. We have heard many sermons *about* Him, but we do not need to know *about* Him. We need to know Him the way He really is: What does He like? What does He dislike? What causes His power to increase in a service? What causes it to decrease, so we can avoid those things. We have to do supernatural experiments in the realm of the Spirit and find out what is most effective.

Supernatural Feats

We are moving into a place in the world that, if the Church does not produce what she has been talking about, she is going to be sawn asunder. No, I am not preaching doom and gloom. I am saying, "Wake up, look, and move."

What is the Church going to do when rock stars and spiritualists come out on stage and say, "*We* are the answer for the world," and perform supernatural feats before the cameras? What is the Church going to do? Are we going to do as the Church did in the past, ignore it and say, "It will go away?" We have said that long enough, and it has not passed away. The only way that kind of thing is going to be destroyed is when a man or a woman of God comes out on the other side of that stage and proclaims, "Our God is greater. Watch this — POW."

For too long, the Church has allowed the world to plunge deeper and deeper into sin. For too long, the preachers have said, "We will preach the Gospel. We will walk in love." The love of God stands up for what is right and proclaims the truth. It is time we got back to that.

It is time we got the Holy Ghost and fire in our bones. Then we will rise up against evil things — not in wondering, not in doubt and unbelief, but in sure confidence that God will show Himself strong.

What are you going to do, Church, when your children, your young people, see those rock stars and spiritualists perform definite miracles by evil power on television?

Some believe that the devil has no power. I am sorry, but that is not the truth. I have seen too many things that the devil has done. I have heard too many true stories about the powers of darkness at work in other countries. Americans do not know what goes on in foreign nations. They have not yet experienced the confrontation with evil that Africans and Europeans have seen.

The Holy Spirit has spoken to me, and to other men of God that in this day and time, America is under the greatest attack of the enemy she has ever seen, and it is going to grow stronger and stronger. A standard must be raised up. A people of power must come forth who will say, "Our God is still Almighty."

Several months ago, a preacher with a little group behind him, egging him on, brought in newspapermen as he prayed for people who had been given up to die. His plan fell through: The sick people did not get healed. What a mockery against the Church. It hurt my heart. I know this kind of thing is coming back to the Church, but we do not need disaster cases.

I went to prayer and said, "God, I know Your Word is true. Why did this man fail?"

And the Lord spoke to me and said, "Those people were trying to build a reputation for their church and their ministry. They were trying to make themselves known."

When you take on warfare like that, you have to make sure that you died to self a long time ago. You have to make sure that you are not in charge, because you are powerless without the Holy Spirit flowing through you. Remember, you do not tell Him what to do. He tells you what to do.

Confrontations Are Coming

I saw a vision when I was preaching at a convention in Tulsa, Oklahoma, in 1984. I saw a stage, and I saw the television networks there taping a confrontation of evil and good. On the stage, I saw the people of the devil and their leaders on one side and the people of God and their leaders on the other side.

The devil's side began to perform miracles and supernatural feats. They would strike someone blind, and the people of God would get them healed. The devil's side would cause someone to be crippled, and one from God's side would say, "Be healed," and the people were healed, one right after the other.

When God vindicates Himself, He does it in a profitable manner. He does not destroy people. He does not kill the flesh. The devil is the one who kills. When God begins to move like this, know that He will not destroy His creation to prove His point. Instead, He will bless it. He will cause it to be greater, because God is a God of greatness and of love.

We are heading toward a place where the people of God must stand up and confront evil forces. The earth is getting increasingly evil, and the kingdom of darkness is getting worse. We must learn how to get in the realm of the spirit and flow with Him so that we will not be left powerless and in doubt and unbelief during the days to come. Instead, we will be full of confidence and faith, and we will say, "Come on, you prophets of Baal. We will show you who has the fire. We will show you whose God reigns."

Those confrontations are coming. When they begin to occur, respect for the Church will return. Men who now slur our God's name will go off our television screens. People in the media will have respect when they see a person of God. Their whole mentality and the way in which they speak to us will change. One reason the world today laughs at the Church, and laughs at you for being a Christian, is because we seem so powerless. We have all the knowledge in the world about chapter and verse, but we had better combine that knowledge with old-fashioned Pentecostal fire in order to go forth and manifest God's power.

When someone doubts God, prove God to him. Let God be real. Let God be manifested in our presence. Let us so walk with the presence of God that miracles happen everywhere we go. Let those who speak against us have their mouths stopped as they watch in amazement the things God does on our behalf. If you will yield yourself to the Holy Spirit, God will turn Heaven and Earth upside down to answer your cry and your prayer.

God's arm is not shortened that He cannot save, and His ear is not deaf that He cannot hear you. Get under the shadow of the Almighty, and go forth proclaiming the good news with signs following.

Preparing for the Future

People have the attitude that the Word will do the work. I understand that, and I believe it. The Word cannot work in the fullness it is supposed to unless the vessel proclaiming it is up to par with God's standard, unless the vessel is full of the Holy Spirit and power, unless he knows the secret of the power of the Holy Spirit (which is yielding), unless self is dead and buried. Unless these qualifications are met, a man or a woman cannot go forth and raise the dead and cause the lost to come to the Lord by the masses.

We stand at a crossroads today. We must make a decision. The things we will go through in the next few years will be preparation and teaching for what is going to come in the future. In the future, the kingdom of darkness is going to be great in the earth, but the Kingdom of Light must be greater and more powerful — and we *must* know what we are doing.

No longer can we play games with God; no longer can we make fun of God and His chosen vessels; no longer can we be in strife; no longer can we dislike our brother or our sister. We have to walk in love, and we have to know what we are doing when the devil confronts the Church of the Living God, saying, "Where is your God?" We have to be able to say, "*Here* He is" — BAM! That is what we need.

We can have all the nice testimonies in the world, but in this day and time, the testimonies may not need to be spoken. Instead, that old-time Holy Ghost fire needs to be delivered from the mouths of God's prophets into the midst of His people. And there needs to come a stirring in the hearts of people that will cause them to go to their prayer rooms once again and fall on their faces, calling on the name of God until He comes down, until He fills their lives to the point that they know they have the power to do what He wants them to do.

Powerless Christians are not worth talking to. Their witness is dead. I have looked at some who go out on witnessing teams, these soul-winning adventures. Yes, they are adventures for the soul-winners, because they never get anybody saved.

You do not have to be eloquent, just have the power to produce. You say, "That's heavy." Well, it is heavy out there. No longer is it "nice" in the world. In the early days of this country, God's people were respected. Then in the 1920s, the Church began to go off into its own world. Christians said, "We will just leave the world to itself. We want to have our bless-me-clubs. Just us four, just rolling around in the Lord." What has happened since the Church has been rolling? The world has taken over.

Look back in history to the time of the crusades. You may not agree with the way the crusaders "spread" the Gospel, but at least the Earth knew there was a Saviour.

The Overcoming Life

In the days to come, God is going to speak to different bands of believers. They will come from different parts of the country, probably not knowing each other, but they will arrive in some city with all of them having the same message from God: "Take ye this city for My glory." They will go through those cities and take them for His glory.

Let the Earth fear the Church of the Lord Jesus Christ. Let the demons fear the faces of the Christians today. Let the kingdom of darkness know your name as Christ's name is known. Let the kingdom of darkness know there are those Christians today who are not frightened to fight. We *are* the victors. We are the overcomers. We are *it* in the Earth today.

Those who persecute us — who speak out against the out-pouring and against those going with the flow of God — will come to nought before too long. They will know that God is in His people. They will know that God is moving in a new way, a way unlike anything you have ever heard or seen before. God's angels will walk hand in hand with the believers, taking on the powers of darkness in combat. We are going to battle, we are going to fight, and we are going to win.

People say, ''You should not talk about the devil.'' Look what happened because you *did not* talk about him — he almost killed you. You do not have to glorify the devil, just recognize the problem and attack it. You cannot ignore the devil, or he will get you every time. You have to say, ''There is the enemy — there is the source of the problem. Come on, let's get the source.'' Take your confessions and prayers, put them right in the face of the devil, and drive him back out of the way.

You have to get that holy anger, you have to get ruthless in this warfare. The Bible says . . . **the kingdom of heaven suffereth violence, and the violent take it by force** (Matt. 11:12). The violent! You have to get rough. You have to get tough. You have to get into this battle with everything you have.

Knowing Your Enemy

Our brothers and sisters who are oppressing us are talking this and talking that, confessing this and dancing to that. They are saying, ''God is good. Hallelujah!'' The entire time, right next to them, is a demon-possessed person doing the same thing. Then they wonder why such-and-such a church that has forty people is having a massive move of God, and nothing is happening in their church of four hundred.

You have to drive out the powers of darkness. The Lord told me not too long ago, "Americans are the greatest nation on the earth today, but they also have one great problem. They are being possessed and oppressed faster than any other nationality on the earth today."

If a demon is in the mind or body of a Christian, it will cramp the Holy Spirit to where He cannot move. When people are bound, they cannot raise their hands and dance up and down the aisles of their churches. They do not know what is wrong, yet they say, "We've got it all together." That is what they think. They have it all "un-together." If they cannot dance up and down the aisles of the churches here, what are they going to do when they get to Heaven?

If you do not believe in fighting devils, what are you going to do when a horde of them comes knocking at your door? Invite them in for supper?

"I just won't answer the door."

Well, they will just come in the window! We should not be ignorant of the devil's devices. We do not need to be frightened, but we do need to know who is our enemy. How can a military force fight an enemy about which it knows nothing? When a war is going on, agents are sent in to study the enemy and see what he is doing. We in the Body of Christ send our spies in, also. There are spiritual spies in the Earth today. They are called prophets, and they are coming to you with a message: "Arise, Church, and take on your armor. Don't let the sun go down on your wrath. Be not in strife with one another, but join yourselves in faith and in unity and seek my face. Go forth."

God talked to me about an army. What is an army for? Are we just going to dress in armor for the sake of wearing armor? God always has a purpose in everything He does. He never does anything just for the sake of doing it.

When He said through the prophet Joel that in the last days there would be an army that would run on the wall and take the cities, that army was not tiptoeing on the wall. That army was in there with swords and shields, knocking the enemy back and possessing the land that belongs to the Kingdom of God. It is time we took back what the devil has stolen. It is time we took back the Earth. The Earth and the fullness thereof belong to the Lord and His joint-heirs. The prosperity of this world belongs to the Church. The land belongs to us. There is no need for anyone to lack or be in despair, because God has given it to us. However, we must rise up in the power of His might, take our armor, go forth into this battle, and reclaim what belongs to the Church.

Jesus Paid for Prosperity

There should be no need for people to beg for thirty minutes to get half a million dollars in an offering. More than enough money should come in. Do you know why believers do not have any money? They have not gotten violent enough to get it. They gripe about some preacher asking them for some money in an offering. If they would just give, the preachers would quit asking.

Dominion over the entire planet originally was mankind's, but we sinned and gave that dominion to the enemy. Then Christ came and took back all the power and the keys from Satan and said to us, "Go ye into all the world and preach the Gospel. Proclaim unto them that this world is the Lord's, and if they want to be in the Kingdom that is going to rule, they need to get on God's side."

It is going to take money to get this earth back. People do not like to hear that, because money is the one thing they have not died to. You do not own your money. In fact, what is a green bill compared to golden streets? Do not gripe about someone who got violent enough to get out of poverty and into prosperity. Do not dare gripe. You should say, "How did you do it? Teach me."

I am totally against sickness and poverty, because I believe with all my heart that Jesus Christ has paid in full for our healing and prosperity. We have to go back and possess what belongs to us. I am not condemning people. I hope that I can stir them to see where we all should be.

After the United States won World War II, its representatives went into the conquered countries and gave them money to rebuild and become normal again. That is what the Church must do, and the dollars, shillings, and pounds must come to the Church. That is one reason God tells us to be prosperous.

God is moving all over the world. We in North America need to start pouring all the extra money we have, after we have paid our bills and have our needs met, into world evangelism. We need to start pouring it into organizations and ministries or even take a vacation and go someplace and preach.

When I was 19 years of age, God sent me to Uganda to preach. After flying some twenty hours, I arrived and had to go straight to the auditorium to address the people. I did not have time to comb my hair or change my clothes. I felt so dirty, but those people were so hungry that they did not mind. They were not concerned about my rumpled clothes. They were not concerned that I was just 19 years old. They did not ask if I was a pastor, if I had a big ministry, or if I was popular. They were only concerned that I had the Word of God to give them. They were just glad I was there. The only thing they asked was, "Teach us about Jesus. Teach us about the Holy Spirit. Teach us about the Gospel, please." That is all they were looking for.

Reclaiming the Territory

We need to get back to the violence of the Gospel. I did not say to get brutal, I said to get violent. We need to look like that cartoon character, Hulk, when we come in with our sword and our shield and our feet shod, and we are glowing from head to foot, saying, "Devil, move over. You are going to get it!"

If he does not move over when you tell him to, give him chapter and verse, and jab him. The day will come when the devil will say, "Well, when (put your own name here) comes, we had better leave." If we can get the Church of the Lord Jesus Christ as a whole to do that, we will kick Satan off the planet. We will tie him up so that he cannot move.

The devil is not going to give the earth back without a fight. No enemy is going to let you take them over, even after they have lost, without some fighting. That is why governments have to send troops in to clear out the territory. We are going to have to clear out the territory, possess it, and rebuilt it.

59

When Jesus comes for the Church, He will be looking for an active Church, a Church that will say, "Yes, we are working. Come on and help us." That is what He is looking for — a Church that is glorious, without spot or wrinkle. You know, one way to get out spots and wrinkles is to work them out.

The day will come when the people of God will rise up and be so powerful that they will invade cities and even nations, and when they leave that city or nation, the powers of the devil will have been so broken that his presence cannot even be seen or felt there anymore. That shall come to pass. It is coming! It is coming! It looks impossible, but my God specializes in impossibilities.

God never gives a vision to any man or woman which that person can achieve in his own human strength. He always gives you something to do that takes every ounce of faith just to believe that He has called you to do it. *That* is a vision. To accomplish the vision, however, you have to be obedient, and you have to move in faith.

That is where we stand today. The pew needs some action, and the pulpit needs some violence. If the pulpit gets some violence, so will the pew. We need to get off our pews and go out into the world that is dying and let people know that there is a God in Israel! Let them know He is not dead, that our God is alive. If they do not believe it, let God do a few miracles, pray in tongues and shout, and they will get saved. They will believe it.

The day is coming when miracles will become almost commonplace where you are. If people say, "No, there is no God," in your presence, you will pray